I Zingari.

Origin—Rise—Progress—Results.

1869.

HARRISON, Bookseller to the Queen,

59, Pall Mall, London

LONDON
HARRISON AND SONS, PRINTERS IN ORDINARY TO HER MAJESTY,
ST. MARTIN'S LANE.

ORIGIN.

When at Cambridge, F. Ponſonby, C. Taylor, W. Bolland, and others, devoted ſome of their leiſure moments to Cricket and Theatricals. Hence ſprung many matches under various names, ſeveral private theatrical meetings, and, finally, the annual Canterbury gatherings, which have now extended over a period of 20 years.

In July, 1845, F. Ponſonby, S. Ponſonby, J. L. Baldwin, and R. P. Long (who under meſmeric influence aſſiſted at the ſéance), found themſelves at ſupper at the Blenheim Hotel. They then and there formed a Club, chriſtened the ſame, framed rules, and the following day informed W. Bolland that he was Perpetual Preſident, and twenty of their friends that they were Members of I Zingari.

ORIGINAL MEMBERS, 1845.

Perpetual Preſident.
Bolland, W.

Annual Vice-Preſident.
Baldwin, J. L.

Biennial Committee.

Bentinck, G.	Nethercote, H. O.	Ponſonby, *Hon.* S.
Morſe, C.	Ponſonby, *Hon.* F.	Taylor, C.

Members.

Broughton, R.	Leſlie, J.	Pickering, W.
Dewing, E. M.	Loftus, *Lord* H.	Pickering, H.
Gambier, *Capt.* G.	Lyon, *Hon.* C.	Randolph, C.
Glamis, *Lord*	Mills, T. B.	Sheppard, J. G.
Hartopp, E.		Welleſley, R.

Treaſurer and Auditor
Grimſton, *Hon.* R.

Liberal Legal Adviſer.
Tom Taylor.

Secretary.
Long, R. P.

JUNE, 1869.

Present Strength of the Club.

Freedoms - - - - -	2
Members - - - - -	89
Agents - - - - - -	55
Half-Play Members - - -	39
Members Unattached - -	61
Candidates for the Asylum - -	41
Chaplain - - - - - -	1

Results.

Won - - - - - -		171
Lost - - - - - -		80
Unfinished	In favour - -	127
	Against - -	80
Ties - - - - - -		2
Tie in both Innings - - -		1
		461

RULES AND REGULATIONS.

AT a Meeting held—no matter when, and much leſs where—

NOBODY, *Chairman.*

The following Rules and Regulations were propoſed and unanimouſly adopted :—

"Reſolved,"

1. That a Club be founded for mutual Cricket accommodation, which ſhall have the name and ſtyle of "I Zingari."

2. That the Club be under the control of a Perpetual President, an Annual Vice-President, and a Biennial Committee of ſix members ſelected by the P.P.

3. That no Candidate be propoſed unleſs ſo agreed at a meeting conſiſting of P.P., A.V.P., and not leſs than two B.C. men. The mode of election as follows:—The Candidate ſhall be placed at a wicket, with or without a bat, as the C. may decide, and be bowled at by

the A.V.P. or by any member of I Z. so deputed by A. V. P. One straight ball to exclude. The number of balls given not to exceed the number of Members comprising I Z.

4. That every Member have the privilege of playing one match during the season, when, upon his producing five names of Members (in addition to his own), who are willing to take part in such match, five other Members shall be bound in honour to make up the team.

5. That the field be under the SOLE control of the Member making the match, or of any Zingaro whom he may depute.

6. That the Entrance be nothing, and the Annual Subscription do not exceed the entrance, but that the expenses of a match (*i.e.* of the I Z. umpire, &c.) be defrayed by the Members engaged therein.

7. That all direction connected with the game *may* be conveyed in the French or Italian languages.

8. THAT NO MEMBER UPON ANY OCCASION PLAY AS AN OPPONENT TO I Z., ANY TRANSGRESSION OF THIS RULE TO ENTAIL IMMEDIATE EXPULSION FROM THE CLUB.

9. That although mirth be acceptable upon all occafions, ill-timed mirth be generally avoided, and that all perfonalities, particularly thofe P. P., be evaded.

10. That the P. P., A.V. P., and not lefs than two B.C. men, be empowered to frame fuch additional rules or regulations as they may deem conducive to the welfare of I Z., provided always that they do not cancel former rules or regulations.

11. That the A.V.P. be empowered to depute a fubftitute in the place of any abfent B.C. man.

12. That the P.P., A.V.P., and not lefs than two B.C. men, be empowered to appoint agents in different parts of the globe, in addition to the eftablished number of regular members.

13. That no agent be fubject to Rule 8.

14. That in future NO queftions of ANY KIND be put to the P.P., A.V.P, or to the Committee.

15. That the number of the Club be limited to......See Rule 14.

RULE 16.

That an Eleven may be ſelected as Candidates, who, *ſibeneſegeſſerint*, may be hereafter elected.

LIST.

Probative and Probable.

Finch, *Hon.* C.
Grimſton, *Hon.* W.
Hartopp, W. E.
Leigh, *Hon.* G. H. C.
Molyneux, Viſcount.
Morſe, C.
Pickering, F.
Ponſonby, Robert.
Randolph, F.
Somerset, Lord E.

Information.

The Committee, anxious to meet the views of the Club in general, and of ſome Members in particular, beg to ſay, ſhould any information be required, the Member or Members deſirous of ſuch information may obtain it (if he or they can) by a written application to the Chairman who preſided at the formation of the Club.

Obſervation.

Rule 8 transgreſſed upon *two occaſions only* —Immediate expulſion the reſult.

Supplication.

Members playing in Zingaric Matches are more than moſt earneſtly requeſted to abſtain from wearing *any* coloured ſhirt, jacket, or trouſers. A Zingaric Belt, Cap, or Ribbon round hat, cap, or neck, ſhould be the only diſtinguiſhing badge.

Irritation.

"Aie ! ! !——There's the rub."

Old Play.

I Z. Bowlers are requefted not to become rubbers of heads, hats, caps, &c., when a ball accidentally paffes near a Wicket.
I Z. Batfmen and Fieldsmen being hit at double or fingle wicket are not entitled to the rub.

Prohibition.

Health Drinking and Dry Toafts

STRICTLY PROHIBITED.

Intimation.

If *abfolutely* unable to keep the " Promife to Play," give timely notice to the head of the Eleven you difappoint.

Abnegation.

Sacrifice self—Confider the interefts of the Club—Your circle of real friends will confiderably increafe.

Reiteration.

Keep your promife—keep your temper—keep your wicket up.

I ZINGARI SONG,

WRITTEN BY

W. BOLLAND, P.P.I Z.

AIR.—*Red. White, and Blue.*

We are told England's armies affembled,
When Liberty's caufe was in view,
We are told too that tyranny trembled,
'Neath the folds of the Red, White, and Blue.
Yes! The Red, White, and Blue o'er the ocean,
Has floated in conquefts of old,
But to-night let us pledge our devotion
To the folds of the Red, Black, and Gold.
CHORUS.—To the folds, &c., &c.

The ball the ftout cricketer urges,
Cleaves a pathway of peace o'er the plain,
The weapon he wields leaves no fcourges,
No record of carnage or pain;
No! 'tis his to cement man's affection,
Reviving his paftime of old.
In our camp then we fear no defection,
From the folds of the Red, Black, and Gold.
CHORUS.—From the folds, &c., &c.

As the eagle fcans defert and mountain,
As the fea-bird the wilds of the deep,
As the water fprings free from the fountain,
And dafhes unbound down the fteep,
So our wandering band fhuns all warning,
In every foil plants its hold,
Each tract of Old England adorning
With the folds of the Red, Black, and Gold.
CHORUS.—With the folds, &c., &c.

Then the wine cup, the wine cup bear hither,
Fill high, we fip nought but the brim,
May the germ we have planted ne'er wither,
Nor the ftar of our birth-right grow dim;
May the friendfhips we have formed never fever,
May each link lengthen long and grow old,
In a bumper, "Here's Cricket for ever,"
'Neath the folds of the Red, Black, and Gold.
CHORUS.—'Neath the folds, &c, &c

1869.

MEMBERS.

HIS ROYAL HIGHNESS THE PRINCE OF WALES.

Amherſt, *Hon.* J G.
Antrobus, R.
Arkwright, C.

Balfour, R.
Barry, A. Smith
Bowmont, *Marquis of*
Boyle, C. E.
Broughton, F.
Burnett, E. W.

Camden, *Marquis*
Coventry, *Earl of*

De Grey, *Hon.* T.
Digby, K. E.
Drake, *Rev.* E. T.
Dyke, W. H.

Ellesmere, *Earl of*
Elphinstone, R. D.
Evetts, W.
Exeter, *Marquis of*

Fellowes, E. L.
Fellows, H.
Fitz Gerald, R. A.
Foljambe, F.
Forester, C. T.
Fryer, F. E. R.

Garnier, T. P.
Gore, F.
Gore, S.
Gosford, *Earl of*
Grimston, W. E.

Guernſey, *Lord*
Gueſt, *Sir* I. B.

Hamilton, *Lord* G.
Hamilton, *Viſcount*
Hopwood, A. R.
Horner, J.
Huntley, *Marquis of*
Hyde, *Lord*

Johnſon, G. R.

Lane, *Rev.* C. G.
Lane, W. W. C.
Langley, F.
Leigh, *Hon.* E. C.
Leigh, *Hon. and Rev.* J.
Lubbock, A.
Lyttelton, *Hon.* C. G.
Lyttelton, *Hon.* Spencer

Maitland, W. F.
March, *Earl of*
Marſhall, *Captain* H.

Marſham, C.
Marſham, *Rev.* C. D.
Marſham, R.
Mayne, C. H.
Methuen, *Hon.* P.
Middleton, W. G.
Mitchell, R. H. A.
M'Cormick, *Rev.* J.
Mordaunt, J.
Mordaunt, *Rev.* O.

Norman, F.

Paget, *Lord* H.
Payne, *Rev.* A.
Payne, A. F.
Pelham, *Hon.* F. G.
Pickering, W. P.
Ponſonby, J. H.
Powell, *Captain* G.
Pratt, *Lord* G.

Queenſberry, *Marquis of*

Ricardo, A.
Royston, *Viscount*
Rose, W. M.
Round, J.

Skelmersdale, *Lord*
Smith, A. L.
Spencer, *Earl*
Stanhope, *Hon.* E.
Stewart, *Captain* H.

Tennent, H. N.
Thesiger, *Hon.* E.
Traill, W.
Tredcroft, E.
Tritton, E. W.
Tritton, W. F.

Villiers, F. E.

Willoughby de Broke, *Lord*
Whymper, F.

AGENTS.

1869.

Allix, N.
Acheſon, *Captain Hon.* E.B.
Arkwright, A. C.

Baillie, *Lieut.-Colonel* D.
Bateſon *Lieut.-Colonel* R.
Bathurſt, *Colonel* F
Bathurſt, A.
Bingham, *Lord.*
Bruen, H.
Buller, C. F.
Buller, *Lieut.Colonel* R.
Byng, C. G.

Campbell, F.
Clayton, *Captain* W. C.
Cole, E.

Denne, *Captain*
Dillon, *Captain Hon.* R. V.
Downe, *Viſcount.*

Edwards, F. I.

Fiennes, *Major Hon.* Ivo de V.

Garlies, *Captain Lord.*
Grey, *Major* G.

Hartopp, *Captain* W.
Hay, *Lieut.-Colonel Hon.* C.
Hill, *Hon.* G.
Honywood, *Sir* C.
Hutchinson, W. F. M.

Inge, J. W.

Kennedy, R. G.
Kingſcote, H. B.
Kington, *Captain* W. N.

Lennox, *Lord* A. G.

McNeile, A. J.
Marſhall, *Colonel* F.
Milles, *Hon.* G.
Milman, *Lieut.-Colonel* G. H.
Montagu, *Hon.* O.
Montagu, *Hon.* V.

Newbolt, *Captain*

Ormonde, *Captain Marqueſs of*
Oſborn, H.

Paget, *Lord* A.
Paget, *Lord* B.

Parnell, *Lieut.-Colonel* W. H.
Peyton, *Captain Sir* A.
Ponsonby, G.

Ricardo, A. L.
Rochfort, H.

Stephens, *Captain* F.
Stewart, *Captain Hon.* A.
Stewart. *Captain* A. C. H.

Traill, *Captain* G.
Tryon, *Captain* R.
Turnour, *Viscount*

Walrond, W. H.
Walton, *Captain*
Williams, *Major*. O. L. C.

Half-Play Members, 1869, liable to be called out.

Archdall, H. M.
Arkwright, J.
Anſon, *Rev.* T. A.

Balfour, A.
Barker, G.
Barton, J. H.
Baillie, W. H.
Blore, *Rev.* E. W.
Boldero, Rev. H. K.
Boldero, *Major*

Cecil, Lord A.
Chitty, J.
Clement, R.

Compton, F.
Creyke, W.

Darnley, *Earl of*
Dickens, *Captain* G.
Ducane, *Rev.* A.

Eaton, C. O.

Fellows, *Rev.* W.
Fiennes, *Hon. and Rev.* C.
Fiennes, *Hon.* J.
Fiennes, *Hon. and Rev.* W.
Fitzwilliam, *Hon.* C.

Harbord, *Captain Hon.* W.

Leigh, Auſten

Molyneux, C. B.

Parker, J. P.
Peel, *Rev.* H.
Pickering, *Rev.* H.

Soames, S.
Stewart, *Hon.* R. H. S.
Streatfield, R.

Taylor, *Lieut.-Colonel* E. T.
Torrens, *Captain* A.
Tottenham, *Captain* A. S.
Tower, *Lieut.-Colonel* H.
Twiſs, Q.

Members unattached to Cricket
but
Attached to I Z.

Alexander, C.
Alexander, J.
Aftley, *Lieut.-Colonel* J.
Aylefford, *Earl of*

Bathe, *Major-General* H. P. de
Bayley, L.
Beaufort, *Duke of*
Bligh, *Hon.* H.
Bligh, *Hon. and Rev.* E.
Bulkeley, R.
Bury, *Vifcount*

Caulfield, Tiny
Charteris, *Hon.* R.

Cheſterfield, *Earl of*
Cliſſold, J.
Cotterell, *Sir* H.
Cockerell, A. P.
Curzon, *Hon.* Richard.
Curzon, *Hon.* Robert

Dalkeith, *Earl of*
Deacon, S.
Dewing, E. M.
Dormer, *Hon.* J.

Ellis, *Hon.* L. A.
Elliſon, C.
Everſfield, C. G.

Fitzhardinge, *Lord*
Fitzwilliam, *Hon.* H.
Forſter, *Colonel* F.

Goodlake, *Lieut.-Colonel* G. L.

Hanbury, O.
Hankey, *Colonel* A.
Harenc, C.
Harewood, *Earl of*
Holmes, T. K.

Kingſcote, *Colonel* N.

Lang, *Rev.* R.
Lanſdowne, *Marquis of*
Laſcelles, *Captain* C.
Leiceſter, *Earl of*
Leſlie, *Colonel* C. P.
Leſlie, J.
Londesborough, *Lord*
Longe, F. D.
Long, R. P.

Macdonald, *Col. Hon.* J. W. B.
Molyneux, *Captain Hon.* C. C
Molyneux, *Hon.* R.
Morgan, H.

Peters, H.
Ponſonby, *Colonel* H.

Reilly, *Lieut.-Colonel* Tim.

Sefton, *Earl of*
Somerſet, *Lord* H.
Stamford, *Earl of*
Strathmore, *Earl of*
Suffield, *Lord*
Sykes, F.

Taylor, Tom
Trevor, *Lord* E. Hill

Vernon, *Lord*
Vyſe, *Captain* F.

Worceſter, *Marquis of*

Candidates for the Afylum for Aged and Decayed Zingari.

Anglefey, *Marquis of*

Baillie, *Colonel* H.
Baldwin, J. L.
Bentinck, G. C.
Bidwell, J.
Bradfhaw, *Rev.* J.
Brougton, R.

Coke, *Lieut.-Colonel Hon.* W.
Craven, W.

Gambier, *Major-General* G.
Grant, *Rev.* F. C. Hope
Grimfton, *Hon.* R.

Hankey, R.
Hartopp, E.
Heneage, *Lieut.-Colonel* M.

Keate, R. W.
Ker, R.
Kinnoull, *Earl of*

Lambert, *Captain* F.
Law, A. P.

Maxwell, *Captain* J. H.
Mayne, H. B.
Micklethwait, F. N.
Mills, *Rev.* T. B.
Moncrieff, *Sir* T.
Morgan, *Hon.* G.
Morſe, C.
Mundy, *Major-General* Pip

Nethercote, H. O.

Ponſonby, *Hon.* F.
Ponſonby, *Hon.* S.

Randolph, *Rev.* C.
Ricardo, F.

Sheppard, J. G.
Stacy, F.
Sutton, R.

Taſwell, *Captain* G.
Taylor, C.
Thackeray, *Rev.* F.
Traill, J.

Whittaker, C.

Yonge, G.

Chaplain.

Hopwood, *Rev.* F.

The Freedom of I Z. was preſented to

Abercorn, *Duke of*
Bayley, *Sir* J.

1869.

OFFICERS OF THE CLUB.

P. P.

A. V. P. Baldwin, J. L.

B. C. M.

Ponſonby, *Hon.* F.
Micklethwait, F. N.
Taylor, C.
Ponſonby, *Hon.* S.
Bentinck, G. C.
Ayleſford, *Earl of*

Secretaries.

Fiennes, *Hon. and Rev.* C.
Leigh, *Hon.* E. C.

Chancellor.

Bayley, *Sir* J.

Liberal Legal Adviſer.

Tom Taylor

Mutual Military Meſsman.

Bathe, *Major-General* H. P. de

Xtraordinary Aide de Camp et Champs.

Macdonald, *Col. the Hon.* J. W. B., *C.B.*

Treaſurer and Auditor.

Grimſton, *Hon.* R.

Late Members.

Anglesey, *Marquis of*
Arkwright, *Captain* H.
Bagot, *Major* G.
Baillie, A.
Balfour, E.
Beauclerk, C.
Bolland, W. P.
Carlisle *Earl of* (Freedom)
Cheslyn, R.
Duff, H. G.
Everard, *Captain* W.
Goring, C.
Hawtrey, *Rev. Dr.* (Freedom)
Heneage, W.
Jolliffe, *Captain* H.
Mayne, *Brigadier*
Mostyn, *Hon.* T.
Oom, A. K.
Oxenden, C.
Pickering, *Rev.* H.
Ponsonby, *Lieut.-Colonel* A.
Ricardo, W.
Strathmore, *Earl of*
Taylor, T. C.
Taylour, *Lord* R.
Vernon, H.
Ward, W.
Wellesley, R.
Westcar, *Captain*

www.ingramcontent.com/pod-product-compliance
Lightning Source LLC
LaVergne TN
LVHW052014160826
845678LV00003B/1045
9780353480025